JOURNEY TO THE HEART OF GRACE

A SELF-LOVE SURVIVAL GUIDE

SHELLY VAN GOEYE

For My Daughters

For the battles you didn't see, the things you couldn't understand, and the moments I didn't get it right…I want you to know I was learning. I was growing, stretching, and doing my best to find my way. Not only for me, but for you.

Thank you for loving me through it.

This book holds pieces of that journey. A trail of healing I leave behind, and a reminder for you to always return to the truth: You are worthy. You are loved. And you never have to earn either one.

This is for you. So you never forget who you are.

And for my husband,

Thank you for believing in me; for supporting not just this book, but the woman who had to rise in order to write it. Your unwavering love gave me space to heal, create, and finally bring this lifelong dream to life.

I love you!

CONTENTS

INTRODUCTION

A year and a half ago, my first essay was published in a multi-author book called *Shine Your Soul Light*. I wrote about the experience that led me to leave my marriage, and the profound opening that followed—one that began a deep, ongoing healing process. At that time, I was a long way from home. I didn't trust my reality, and I didn't trust myself. I felt drained, disconnected, and heartbroken. I was in a toxic, abusive relationship and knew I needed to get out. After ten long years, I finally found the strength and courage to leave.

During that season of my life, I was deeply involved in the church. I've always been curious from a spiritual perspective, and my connection to the Divine was the one thing that kept me going. As a seeker, I constantly questioned things; seeking deeper meaning, understanding, and ways my experiences might help someone else.

Ironically, I was focused on helping others heal, but not necessarily myself. So, I set off to learn.

And in all the learning, I realized how much healing I still needed.

One of the most important revelations was this: *I didn't know how to show up for me.* Somewhere along the way, I had internalized a belief that I didn't matter. My subconscious programming and patterns had been running the show, and I had completely abandoned myself. I was spiritually bypassing my own experience; my emotions, my trauma, and my internal chaos.

Spiritual Bypassing: *Sometimes, in our search for healing, we use spiritual ideas to cover up rather than confront our wounds. True grace invites us to face ourselves with honesty and tenderness, not escape our own hearts.*

To quiet the noise, I started creating safe, still spaces to heal. I began withdrawing from anything that created more confusion—church being one of them. I was angry. Not at God, but at the idea of God that the church had given me.

One of the safest spaces I found was through journaling. The blank page became a sanctuary, a place where I could pour out everything that was going through my mind. As I wrote, I began to reconnect with my own heart. Over time, this practice became a bridge reconnecting me to Spirit in a more direct, intimate way. The guidance I received on the page was the same Source I had been praying to all along. In many ways, my journaling became a sacred form of prayer. Some of the most beautiful insights I received were about Grace. They felt like a warm embrace. Healing and so transformative.

Recently, my guides whispered that it was time to write a book. I knew instantly they were talking about *this* book —*the Grace book.* What I didn't know then was that the original title would shift and the message would deepen. So, I said yes. Because I sensed that writing this book wouldn't just be healing for others, it would be a vital step in my own healing, as well.

Another practice that has helped me reconnect with my inner world, and with Spirit, is guided meditation. In one recent journey, I found myself entering the Akashic Records; a place I've visited before, though usually with only fleeting impressions. This time was different. I found myself in a beautiful room, standing on a large circular platform, surrounded by shelves of books and bathed in radiant white light. All around me were figures; some appearing only as a presence, others as soft silhouettes. I felt a sense of awe as I realized these were my guides, angels, and master teachers; my spiritual support team.

They signaled for me to turn around. Behind me was a podium with an open book resting on it. A book I was not yet allowed to access. I asked what it was. Was it the book of my life? They didn't answer directly but told me this: *"We are always with you. We are always guiding and supporting you. However, you must ask us for help."*

So, out of curiosity, I asked.

"What's in the book? What do I need to know?"

Their response was simple:

"You need to learn self-love."

Ok...self-love. I know about that. I thought to myself.

Then I heard:

"It's not enough to understand it. You must embody it. Only then will you be ready to see what's inside the book."

There it was. My next assignment.

Embody self-love.

My journey toward embodying self-love has been just that—a journey. It hasn't been linear, and it hasn't always been easy. I've had to put the pieces of myself back together slowly, gently, and lovingly. As I write this book, I'm still on that journey. I'm walking it with you. Just like my guides said—it's not enough to know self-love. We must live it. Breathe it. Choose it. Every single day.

However, there's a reason so many of us struggle to do that.

A Note on Unlearning

For many of us, the word Grace carries weight. We were told it was something bestowed from above, and only if we were good enough, quiet enough, selfless enough. We were taught to seek forgiveness, but not to forgive ourselves. To love our neighbor, but not ourselves. To surrender, but never to receive.

Some of these messages came wrapped in scripture, tradition, or the teachings of well-meaning faith communities. Yet when Grace becomes a transaction; something you must earn, beg for, or suffer through; it stops being Grace.

This book is a tender unlearning.

The heart of G.R.A.C.E.—Gentleness, Reverence, Acceptance, Compassion, and Empathy—is here to invite you home. Not to a church, a doctrine, or someone else's idea of who you should be. But to your own soul. To your body. To your voice. To your sacred, untamed, and fully loved self.

These are not commandments. They're companions. Not rules, but rituals of remembrance.

They'll walk beside you as you rewrite the stories that once kept you small. And together, they'll help you remember the truth that never left:

Grace was never about being worthy enough to receive.
It's about realizing you were never unworthy
in the first place.

This book, *Journey to the Heart of Grace*, is an expression of the wisdom shared with me on those pages. It is an inner journey written for you; the one who longs to come home to herself. It's a safe space. A container where unconditional love and support reside, and a place for you to reconnect to your own heart.

My prayer is that it will shine *truth* on your inner light, and help you remember who you are and what you're here to accomplish.

Beautifully Empowered. Perfectly imperfect.

Held in Grace.

PART I

PREPARING FOR THE JOURNEY

Grace lives inside of you already.
True Grace isn't something to earn or reach for: it's the
self-love and wholeness you are meant to embody.
This is not a search. It's a return.
Let's begin.

WHAT IS GRACE?

After deciding to write this book, the concept of *Grace* moved to the forefront of my awareness. I began noticing how often the word appears in everyday conversation; and more importantly, what people seem to *mean* when they use it. I started listening beneath the words.

I heard things like:

- "I want to age gracefully."
- "I want to navigate transitions with Grace."
- "Can you, please, just grant me some grace right now?"
- "We are saved by God's Grace."
- "Grace, and Grace alone, will set us free."

Sometimes the word shows up in spiritual conversations about healing, like a sacred placeholder - important, but undefined.

A friend recently asked what I was writing about. When I said *Grace*, she paused, looked off into the distance, and said thoughtfully, "Now *that is* a concept to contemplate." Then she mentally floated away.

Her response made me wonder: *How many of us have carried the word Grace in our vocabulary, but never stopped to explore what it actually means to us?*

Let's take a closer look at some of the ways we use it.

"I want to age gracefully."

When someone says this, they're often referring to aging with class, beauty, and ease. They don't want to age looking 'harsh' or 'weathered.' They want the process to be gentle. Aging, of course, looks different for each of us. But behind this statement is a longing for kindness toward ourselves as we change, rather than self-criticism or shame.

"I want to navigate transitions with Grace."

This suggests a desire to move through life's inevitable changes with flow and steadiness. It makes me think about the *energetics* of Grace—how it *moves*.

Navigating grief, uncertainty, endings, or new beginnings can be difficult. What we're really asking for is softness.

Smoothness. The sense that we're being carried, not dragged. Held, not battered, in the storm.

"Can you please just grant me some grace right now?"

This is a vulnerable request for leniency, for space, for understanding. A plea for forgiveness or a pause when things feel heavy or overwhelming.

It's asking, "Can I be human for a moment? Can I not be perfect? Will you still hold me gently?" Even just imagining being met with that kind of Grace brings a sense of exhale.

"We are saved by God's Grace."

Here's where I take a deep breath.

This is one of the most common, and complicated, ways Grace is referenced in Christian culture. Grace has its own theological framework in many churches.

When I was immersed in that world, we spoke of Grace as if it was universally understood, but if you asked me to define it... I couldn't quite put it into words. I tried, of course; quoting doctrine or repeating what I'd heard:

"Grace is God's unmerited favor."

But something inside me always felt like that fell short.

It was something I could feel but not explain.

To me, true Grace is something far more intimate.

It's not about religious worthiness. It's not something we earn or something we beg for.

Grace is the presence that holds you when everything falls apart.

It's the gentle whisper that says, *"You don't have to fix yourself to be loved."*

Grace is the soft space between judgment and acceptance, between pain and peace.

It's the love that keeps reaching for you even when you've stopped reaching for yourself.

To me, Grace is like a body of water; warm, flowing, alive.

It doesn't push or demand.

It surrounds you, supports you, moves you gently toward the shore even when you're too tired to swim.

It reminds you: *You're not alone.*

When Grace Gets Distorted

But what if you've spent years in a toxic environment; whether in a relationship, a community, or a church?

What if the word Grace was used more like a weapon than a balm?

This is where things get tender.

Some of my deepest wounds came from the spiritual spaces I trusted the most. I was taught that Grace was unconditional, but the message also held an unspoken expectation. One that said: I had to be good, obedient, humble, repentant, self-sacrificing.

I was taught to be small.

To deny myself.

To carry shame as a sign of devotion.

This kind of Grace kept me disconnected from my own intuition.

It made me feel like my voice, my body, and my boundaries didn't matter.

That my suffering somehow made me more righteous.

That version of Grace didn't save me. It silenced me.

It wasn't until I left that world and began rebuilding a relationship with the Divine on *my own terms* that I started to experience true Grace.

It came softly; in ways I didn't expect.

It came in quiet moments; through breath, through journaling, through nature.

Through learning to forgive myself.

Through learning to stay with my feelings.

With my body.

With the parts of me I was taught to abandon.

To stay present instead of shutting down.

To stay open instead of closing off.

To stay connected to myself, even when it was hard.

That's where I found Grace.

So, what is Grace?

Grace is not about deserving.

It's not about striving.

It's not about performance.

Grace is the birthright you forgot you had.

Given by the Divine; not for being good, but simply for being. It's not a prize to earn, but your soul's quiet inheritance.

Somewhere along the way, you were taught to question your worth. But Grace was never lost; only buried beneath the noise.

Beneath the shame.

Beneath the stories that said you weren't enough.

Grace is a container that surrounds you.

She envelops you like a fluffy pillow; soft, comforting, and supportive.

She's the one who catches you when you fall and holds you when things fall apart.

She is safe. She is trustworthy.

She is always here.

When Grace turns inward, she becomes Self-Love.

The kind that says, *"You matter. You are enough. You don't have to earn this."*

Let me also say this:

I've been in a lot of toxic relationships and steeped in toxic teachings from the church.

I have a gift: I'm deeply sensitive, intuitive. I see beyond the surface. I can often sense the intent behind someone's words or actions, even when they're clumsy, cold, or confusing.

But that gift came with a cost.

I made excuses for people who didn't have the capacity or the willingness to be honest, take accountability, or reflect on how their behavior affected others. I kept seeing the best in them, even when they had no intention of changing.

I gave Grace where I should have drawn boundaries.

Over and over, I made space for their humanity... while quietly abandoning my own.

When we grant too much Grace to people or systems that harm us, we begin to lose ourselves.

We blur the line between compassion and self-erasure; the slow, quiet process of silencing our truth, minimizing our needs, or making ourselves invisible in the name of being "loving" or "good."

We start calling survival *patience,* and pain *purpose.*

And if we're not careful, we become trapped in a cycle of victimhood mistaking our tolerance of poor treatment for spiritual strength.

We tell ourselves we're being loyal, kind, or faithful. When in reality, we're tolerating harm and calling it Grace.

True Grace is not martyrdom.

It's not the act of sacrificing yourself over and over to prove your goodness, your loyalty, or your love.

Martyrdom says: *"I'll stay, I'll suffer, I'll shrink so you don't have to change."*

Grace says: *"I can love you and still choose myself."*

Martyrdom is rooted in fear and old conditioning; the belief that love must be earned through suffering.

Grace is rooted in truth. She honors both compassion and boundaries. She knows your needs, your voice, your well-being... all matter.

Grace doesn't ask you to abandon yourself in the name of being "good."

She invites you to come home to yourself.

True Grace honors your boundaries as sacred.

She holds others accountable—and holds you close.

In this book, we'll explore Grace through five sacred elements:

Gentleness, Reverence, Acceptance, Compassion, and Empathy.

Each one is an invitation to unlearn the lies, reclaim your truth, and return to your own heart.

You're not reading this by accident.

Something in you is ready.

The map is within you. Let's begin to unfold it.

Reflection: Meeting Grace

Before you gather your tools for the journey, take a few moments to pause here. You don't need anything special —just a quiet space, a pen, and a willingness to listen inward.

Let this be your first entry. The beginning of your return.

Use the following questions to gently explore what Grace means to you—before anyone else defines it for you.

1. *What is your earliest memory or experience of the word "Grace"? Was it comforting? Confusing? Complicated? What associations does it still carry?*
2. *In what areas of your life have you been offering Grace to others but withholding it from yourself?*
3. *Have you ever mistaken endurance or suffering for love, loyalty, or spiritual strength? How did that feel in your body? In your heart?*
4. *If Grace is your birthright, your soul's quiet inheritance, what parts of you are ready to remember that now?*
5. *What would it look like to come home to yourself today?*

Is there a small step, gesture, or truth you can honor right now?

Let your answers be imperfect. Let them surprise you.

Grace is already unfolding.

AN INVITATION &
REMEMBRANCE

Dare

By Shelly Van Goeye

What do you think you are going to lose?
I dare you...
Reach down and untie your shoes.
Brush fear and uncertainty out of your way.
Explore the possibilities of each new day.
Cut every string that binds up your mind.
Release the emotions.
Begin to unwind.
Jump out of the box you've placed yourself in.
Unveil the adventure waiting within.
Excitement, fulfillment is waiting for you.
Reach down...
Untie...
Step out of your shoes!

This poem is more than a childhood dare; it's a soulful invitation.

An invitation to loosen the knots of fear and doubt...

To untangle the mental and emotional strongholds that keep you playing small...

To remember who you are beneath the conditioning and the shoulds.

You are a divine being, here to leave your mark on the world.

You are here to learn, grow, and become all that your heart longs to be.

This isn't a journey toward a distant destination.

It's a return.

A return to the inner path that has always been within you.

A pilgrimage to the heart of Grace; where self-love, truth, and deep acceptance dwell.

This is a journey of courage, curiosity, and transformation.

You are invited to loosen the grip of old fears, step beyond your comfort zone, and explore the vast landscape of your soul.

Grace is not a reward you must earn.

It's a presence already waiting for you.

All that's required is your willingness to receive it.

So...

Are you ready and willing to take the first step?

The Park Bench of Indecision (a.k.a. Procrastination)

Most of us, at some point in life, find ourselves standing at a crossroads. If you haven't yet, trust me, you will. And let's be honest, it's not usually a place we enjoy. Crossroads often appear when something in our life is no longer working. By *not working*, I mean there's a misalignment. Something just doesn't feel right, and the path we've been walking no longer seems to lead where our soul wants to go.

Sometimes, when we arrive at these moments, the way forward is clear. We know what to do, and we feel ready to do it.

But other times? The decision feels *enormous*. Life-changing and somewhat terrifying.

We're faced with a choice: stay with the familiar... or step into the unknown.

"The unknown? No, thank you!"

I hear you. I see you. I've *been* you. Many times.

In fact, I know this place so intimately that I built a bench beneath the shade of some tall, compassionate trees and named it:

The Park Bench of Indecision.

There's even a plaque on it that reads:

"In honor of those to come. You are not alone."

At one point in my life, I parked myself there for a decade.

Ten years believing I could keep walking the same path and somehow create a different outcome. Ten years circling back to the same fork in the road. Over and over, I'd sit on that bench, talk myself into staying with the known, and convince myself it would be different *this* time.

But it never was.

Eventually, the pain of staying where I was grew louder than the fear of the unknown.

I needed a Divine shove.

Here's what I've learned:

You always have the opportunity to choose your path.

Every day, in both small and significant ways, you choose.

And sometimes? *Not* choosing, just sitting, is a choice too.

I don't say this with judgment, but with love. With awareness gained through experience.

The choices we delay or avoid often end up costing us more than we realize.

And sometimes, life has to ache a little more deeply before we're ready to move. That pain becomes our permission slip to choose differently.

Looking back, part of me wishes I hadn't waited ten years.

But that decade taught me.

It shaped me.

It carved out the space where Grace could eventually take root.

I had to walk that loop long enough to recognize I was worthy of something more.

Had I known then what I know now, I might've trusted myself sooner.

So maybe you're standing at a crossroad right now.

Or maybe you've been resting on your own Park Bench of Indecision.

Wherever you are, I want you to know this:

You are not alone.

Take a deep breath. You found this book for a reason. Something in you already said *yes*.

Trust that.

Trust *you*.

And consider this moment…

your first step down a new path.

A Spiritual Being Having a Human Experience

Before we begin packing our Soul Satchel, there's one vital truth to remember:

You are not a human being trying to become more spiritual.

You are a spiritual being, already whole, already sacred having a human experience.

However, this is not the truth many of us were taught.

We were told, sometimes directly, sometimes silently, that we were flawed.

That we had to strive for holiness.

That our bodies were weak.

That our emotions were sinful.

That our pain was proof we had fallen short of God's love.

We were taught to mistrust our desires, suppress our feelings, and be ashamed of our humanity.

We were told to shrink ourselves into obedience, not expand into our fullness.

But this is not the truth of Grace.

You are not a flawed human trying to earn divine favor.

You are a spiritual being who chose to embody a human experience.

You came here to learn, to grow, to feel, to remember.

To taste the full texture of life on Earth; the beauty and the ache, the joy and the heartbreak, the longing and the love.

In the spiritual realm, you did not know hunger.

You did not grieve.

You did not ache or rejoice the way you do here.

But here, in this body, on this Earth, you do.

And that is not a mistake. It's a miracle.

You are here not to escape your humanity, but to *integrate* it with your divinity.

To walk as both; feet on the earth, spirit intact, heart wide open.

Grace does not demand perfection.

It does not wait for you at the end of your healing journey. It walks with you in the messy middle.

It honors the bravery it takes to live inside a body and carry a soul at the same time.

So, as you prepare for this journey, do not pack the old belief that you are too much, too flawed, too emotional, or too broken.

Instead, carry truth. Carry tenderness.

To help you carry this truth forward, I've created a printable version of this Soul Truth. You can paste it into your journal or post it somewhere visible in your daily life. Link and QR below.

https://www.journeytotheheartofgrace.com/

Soul Truth

You Are a Spiritual Being Having a Human Experience
You are not a flawed human trying to earn divine favor.
You are a spiritual being—already whole, already sacred
—having a human experience.
You came here to learn.
To grow.
To feel.
To remember.
To taste the full texture of life on Earth;
the beauty and the ache,
the joy and the heartbreak,
the longing and the love.
You are here not to escape your humanity,
but to integrate it with your divinity.
To walk as both;
feet on the earth,
spirit intact,
heart wide open.
Grace walks with you in the messy middle.
It honors the bravery it takes to live inside a body
and carry a soul at the same time.

Use this truth to guide you when you forget who you are.
Tape it to your mirror. Tuck it in your journal. Let it
speak for Grace when you cannot find the words.

WHAT TO PACK

YOUR SOUL SATCHEL

E very sacred journey begins with intention.

Not the kind we scribble down once and forget, but the kind we set with our whole being.

When we begin a journey of this depth, we do so with care, with clarity, and with soul. Like any traveler preparing for a meaningful voyage, we need to pack; not bags full of clothes or supplies, but inner tools to sustain and support us along the way.

Think of this as your Soul Satchel: a sacred, symbolic bundle of inner wisdom and resources that you'll carry with you as you journey inward.

We choose only what nourishes us, what anchors us, what reminds us of who we truly are. Each item placed in your satchel serves a purpose, not materially, but spiritually.

What you carry matters. What you leave behind matters even more.

Together, we'll gather the soul tools you'll need, each one a reminder of your inner wisdom, as you begin this sacred return to yourself.

Your Inner Compass

Every journey asks us to stay attuned, not just to the road ahead, but to the wisdom within.

You don't need a map with all the answers.

But you *will* need a compass that knows your soul; one that leads you back to your heart.

Your True North is your spirit.

It is the wise, intuitive voice within you, steadfast, steady, *and* rooted in your deepest truth.

It's not a rigid direction. It's not a fixed point.

It's a *living* relationship with the most authentic version of you; the part that whispers, nudges, and resonates.

It shows up as knowing. As longing. As resistance or release.

Even when you lose sight of the path, your inner compass lovingly recalibrates and says:

"This way, beloved."

Setting Your Compass to True North

Before we continue packing, let's pause and turn inward.

You've just reconnected with your Inner Compass; your True North. Now it's time to attune to it.

This guided meditation is an invitation to embody what you've just read, to begin listening inwardly, and to cultivate trust in your own inner knowing. This compass is not a tool you have to learn, it's a truth you already carry.

You'll find the meditation written out on the next page, but I also encourage you to experience it as it was intended: with your eyes closed, your body relaxed, and your heart open. At the end of this chapter, you will find QR and weblink of a free downloadable version for you to listen to.

Let the sound of my voice guide you, just as your inner compass will continue to guide you; gently, steadily, and always from within.

When you're ready... begin.

Guided Meditation

Before you start, find a quiet space where you can sit or lie down comfortably.

Let yourself be undisturbed for a few minutes.

Close your eyes. Breathe deeply. Let the outside world fall away.

Let's take a few moments to become familiar with your Inner Compass; to get to know it better, and to seek its guidance.

This compass is the direction of your highest self and your highest purpose.

Inhale calm and clarity. Exhale any doubt or distraction.

Let your body settle into stillness, Let your mind soften, Let your breath guide you inward.

Now, imagine yourself standing at the edge of a vast, open landscape. The sky stretches endlessly above you. The ground beneath you is solid and supportive.

Take a moment to look around;

Notice the color of the sky, The shape of the clouds, The feeling of wind brushing your skin.

Feel the earth under your feet. Sense the smell of the ground, the plants, the life around you.

Let yourself feel these words: I am exactly where I need to be.

With every breath, your body softens. Tension begins to melt away. Your awareness deepens. Feel the gentle rhythm of your breath. The steady beat of your heart.

Begin to sense the presence deep within you; the part that knows the way, even when the path ahead seems unclear.

Now, visualize a golden compass resting in the palm of your hand. This compass is unique to you; created from the essence of your soul. It is not borrowed. It is not learned.

It is born of you. It glows softly, pulsing with a quiet, steady light.

This is your True North; your inner guidance system. It always points toward self-love, authenticity, and grace.

Hold the compass close to your heart. Feel its warmth radiating through you. Let it sync with your breath, your energy, your deepest truth. Let it attune to you.

Now ask:

What do I need most as I begin this journey?

What do I need to carry with me?

What am I ready to leave behind?

What wisdom do you have for me today?

You may sense a word, an image, a sensation...

Whatever arises, trust it. There is no right or wrong. Only what is true for you in this moment.

Let it settle into your being. Let it root you in clarity and purpose.

Now, envision a path unfolding before you, lit by the gentle glow of your compass.

With each step, imagine fear, doubt, and old expectations falling away like leaves in the wind, drifting out of sight.

These are the stories and beliefs that once held you back. They do not define you. They do not belong to this path.

Step by step, you feel lighter. Freer. More at home in your own body. More at peace in your own soul.

You are not lost. You have never been lost. Your True North has always been within you, waiting to be seen, heard, and trusted.

Take another deep breath…and gently bring the compass back to your heart space.

Feel its glow aligning with your heartbeat; a soft merging of truth and tenderness, anchoring you into the wisdom that lives within.

Know that your True North is always accessible.

It is not a place you must reach; it is a presence you can return to, again and again.

Take another breath in...and thank this part of you for its wisdom,

for its quiet guidance, and for the gift of its everlasting presence.

When you are ready...gently bring your awareness back to your body. Wiggle your fingers and toes. Take one final, grounding breath.

You are ready for this journey. Your compass is set.

Your True North is within you; steady, wise, and deeply devoted to your soul's becoming.

Reflection Prompt

Open your journal and take a few moments to reflect on your experience. Let the insights from this journey move through your pen.

- *What did you discover in this meditation?*
- *What messages or sensations did your True North offer?*
- *What do you feel called to carry forward?*

There's no need to interpret everything perfectly; just write what feels right for you.

Let this be a space for honesty, curiosity, and gentle self-connection.

Your Passport

Every traveler needs a place to record what they discover along the way. This journey is no different.

You won't just be collecting facts or checking off destinations.

This journey inward is a sacred return to your heart.

What you gather along the way will be subtle, symbolic, and soul-deep. This is why you'll need your Passport; two sacred companions to help you document your journey:

- **A Writing Journal** – a place to reflect on prompts, explore your inner terrain, respond to questions, and speak your truth onto the page.
- **An Art Journal** – a visual space to capture the essence of your journey. Here you can draw, collage, stamp, doodle, ore simply mark the moments that move you.

These journals are not assignments.

They are sanctuaries.

They are places to witness your own becoming.

They don't ask for perfection.

They ask for presence.

They are not about proving anything.

They are about revealing what is real.

Your *Writing Journal* helps untangle what's stirring inside.

- It listens when you need to speak.
- It speaks when your truth is ready to rise.
- It helps you slow down, stay present, and become your own mirror.

Your *Art Journal* allows you to express what words cannot.

- It gives shape to emotions through color, mark-making, symbols, and movement.
- Creating art balances the brain, calming the nervous system, reducing stress, and helping you access inner clarity when logic falls short.
- It can quiet the noise so solutions can rise gently to the surface.

Think of it as the illuminated pages of your Passport.

You don't need to be an artist. You don't need to get it "right."

It's a scrapbook for your soul, a space where memory becomes art, and meaning finds form.

It helps you remember what matters without needing to flip through pages of writing to find it.

While you won't find specific art journaling prompts in this book, that part of the journey isn't forgotten, this is just the beginning.

In the future, I'll be offering companion resources, workshops, recorded classes, or even a guided art journal to support this process more deeply.

For now, let your own wisdom lead. As you read, feel, and reflect, you may find images, colors, or symbols rising within you.

Trust them.

Create from them.

Let them move through your hands and into form.

Together, these two journals will help you:

- Hear what you haven't heard before
- See yourself more clearly
- Witness your transformation
- And remember that healing is not only possible —it is already happening

There is no *"right"* way to journal. Only your way.

When in doubt, write it out. When overwhelmed, make a mark. Draw a shape. Let color speak for you.

Your Passport will become a sacred keepsake; a living record of who you are becoming. That's why I invite you to begin now. They are your companions for this journey and they'll help your inner compass speak.

If you're wondering whether this practice will truly matter, or if journaling can really become a source of healing and guidance;

Let me share a story from my own journey. Because I didn't always trust this process either.

In fact, it started with resistance, doubt, and a bookstore whisper I almost ignored.

A Story from My Own Journey

Journaling has been one of the most powerful tools on my own healing path.

Not just as a way to track my thoughts but as a way to truly meet myself.

It helped me listen when I was numb.

It helped me release when I was stuck.

It helped me hear the deeper voice within; the one that always knew where I was going, even when I didn't.

But like many of us, I didn't start out trusting that voice or knowing how to write my way back to it.

This is my story.

It's where the journey truly began for me; messy, reluctant, and cracked wide open.

After my first marriage ended, I found myself in the raw, uncertain space of healing. I was grieving, untethered, and—if I'm honest—angry with God. At the same time, I was beginning to feel the pull of something deeper, a knowing that my own healing journey might one day help others.

During this season, I was enrolled in my first coaching certification program and had just reconnected with one of my lost loves: lampworking (glassblowing in a torch). When some of my classmates found out, they asked if I'd ever read a book called *The Artist's Way*. I hadn't. It sounded interesting, so I tucked the name into the back of my mind.

A few weeks later, my youngest daughter, who wasn't usually my "reader," asked if I'd take her to the bookstore. We were already out running errands, so I said yes.

I usually had a list of titles to hunt down, but that day, I didn't. I wandered aimlessly, open to suggestions.

As I stood in one of the aisles, I paused and asked myself, *what should I get today?*

Much to my surprise, I heard a response.

It was that familiar voice; the one I've come to recognize as my inner guidance, my compass. The voice that shows up over my left shoulder and whispers in just the right moment.

It said, *The Artist's Way.*

I smiled. *Of course!* I remembered the recommendation.

But I didn't know who wrote it, or where to find it. I hadn't even started looking when I glanced at the shelf right in front of me…

There it was.

One copy. Waiting.

I picked it up, started thumbing through it and then I saw the word *God.*

And just as quickly, I snapped it shut and shoved it back on the shelf.

Nope. I am NOT reading another book about GOD.

The voice, patient as ever, came again.

Pick it up.

I scoffed. *"I am not buying this!"* I mumbled under my breath.

I stomped my foot like a child. Thumbed through it again.

Put it back. Again.

I'm sure anyone watching thought I'd lost my mind.

The voice said one more time,

Take it home. You can return it if you don't want it.

With full dramatic flair, I yanked it off the shelf, marched to the checkout counter, and paid for it—disgusted.

But the voice, my guide, my compass knew better.

When I got home, I opened the preface and began to read. Within minutes, I had chills.

The words aligned with exactly where I was emotionally, spiritually, creatively. It didn't preach. It offered possibility.

And then I saw it:

The author used "God" as an acronym: Good Orderly Direction.

Now *that* was a God I could get behind.

One of the core practices in the book is called *Morning Pages;* a daily ritual of writing three longhand pages in your journal first thing in the morning. The author claimed that by page two, your resistance would wear off and creativity would begin to flow.

So, I tried it. I committed to the practice for three months.

There were days I couldn't stop at three pages.

So much poured out of me.

It was the first time in my life I had given myself 30 minutes of undivided attention.

Attention that was needed to reconnect with myself, with my body, my grief, my heart.

Tears came.

Emotions I'd stuffed down for years began to release.

Something sacred opened.

It became a lifeline back to the Divine.

Eighteen years later, I'm still writing.

It helps me untangle the chaos in my mind.

It gives shape to what is asking to be created or healed.

It reveals patterns. It speaks truth.

Sometimes, it opens a channel, and I become a vessel for words that aren't even mine.

This book—*Journey to the Heart of Grace*—was born from that space.

So, as you begin this chapter of your own becoming, know that your journal is more than a notebook.

It's a threshold.

A place to meet yourself again and again with honesty, with curiosity, and with compassion.

You don't have to know what to write.

You don't have to know what will unfold.

Just begin.

Let the ink lead.

Let the page hold you.

Let your Passport become the living archive of your return. As your words begin to unfold on the page, something else will begin to unfold within you; the courage to see yourself clearly.

Because this journey asks not only for your voice...but for your vision.

Binoculars (Not Rose-Colored Glasses)

Leave the rose-colored glasses behind.

This is not a journey of denial or false positivity.

This is a path of truth-telling, clarity, and courageous self-honesty.

To truly experience Grace, you must be willing to see yourself clearly; not through the lens of old wounding or perfectionism, but through the compassionate eyes of truth.

Bring your binoculars.

Bring your willingness to observe without judgment, to examine the beliefs and patterns that no longer serve you, and to witness what is rising within you with love and curiosity.

Binoculars give us perspective. They help us focus on what matters while still holding the larger landscape in view.

They help us navigate unfamiliar inner terrain with awareness and intention.

This journey will ask for your presence, not your performance.

It will ask you to look again, and then again with softer eyes and an open heart.

Let the clarity you gain become part of your liberation.

Let your vision be refined by truth, not distorted by fear.

Now that you're seeing clearly, what happens when what you see feels heavy, painful, or overwhelming?

Your Emergency Survival Kit - G.R.A.C.E

For the Moments You Forget How to Love Yourself

What if Grace '*the energy of Grace*' embodied Gentleness, Reverence, Acceptance, Compassion, and Empathy?

What if this beautiful energy wasn't something you had to earn, chase, or prove yourself worthy of...

But something that could *cover* you? Hold you?

Remind you that you're already enough?

What is Grace was the light that pulls you from the ashes, not because you did everything right, but because you are already worthy of rising?

Instead of beating yourself up for being human, what if you offered yourself this light?

How would your relationship with yourself begin to shift?

Could you begin to heal in a new way with tenderness instead of judgment?

Could you begin to release the shame you carry?

Could you begin to receive the goodness waiting for you?

Could you begin to believe that you matter?

And if your relationship with the Divine has been wounded or weighted down by shame?

Could Grace begin to rewrite that story, too?

Every soul traveler, no matter how seasoned, will face moments when the path disappears beneath their feet.

Times when fear, shame, grief, or exhaustion flood the heart, and it feels easier to turn back, hide, or numb.

That's when the *Emergency Grace Kit* becomes your lifeline.

This isn't about fixing or forcing your way forward.

It's about remembering; remembering who you are, what you carry, and how to hold yourself when you forget.

Inside this kit, you'll find more than tools. You'll find tenderness. You'll find your way back to Grace.

Each item in your Emergency Grace Kit is tethered to one of the Five Elements of Grace, guiding you back into alignment when life feels off center.

These are the five soul-questions to return to when you feel yourself unraveling:

Gentleness

Where do I need to be gentle right now? Am I being

treated with loving-kindness or gentleness; by myself or others?

Gentleness is your soft landing. In times of inner turmoil, ask yourself this question and breathe. So often, we've been conditioned to respond to our pain with pressure, criticism, or productivity. Instead, respond with a pause. With a whisper of kindness. With the simple act of placing your hand over your heart and saying, "It's okay to feel this."

Reverence

Am I honoring myself in this moment? Am I being treated with the respect I deserve?

Reverence reminds you that you are sacred, even when you feel broken. Even when you're on the bathroom floor. This question calls you back to self-honoring. It helps you reclaim your worth when others may not see it, or when you've momentarily forgotten it yourself. Your dignity is non-negotiable. Reverence restores it.

Acceptance

What needs to soften for me to accept the parts of me I am rejecting?

Sometimes, we fight our feelings, our stories, our scars. Acceptance doesn't ask us to like everything, but it does ask us to *face* it. To soften our grip. To welcome even the messy, hurting, and lost parts of ourselves as part of the whole. When you feel fragmented, this question opens the door for wholeness to return.

Compassion

Am I treating myself with tenderness and embracing all of my imperfections?

Compassion is not a performance. It's presence. It's choosing to sit with your sadness instead of silencing it. This question invites you to hold your humanity with gentle hands. To remember that your struggles don't make you less worthy, they make you exquisitely real.

Empathy

Can I witness my own pain without judgment? Can I truly listen to what I need?

Empathy is the sacred act of listening to yourself. When emotions rise like waves, empathy becomes your anchor. It doesn't try to fix the tide. It simply says, *"I'm here. I see you. I hear you."* This question brings you back into relationship with yourself without trying to rush or rescue, only to witness.

These questions are more than prompts. They are portals.

When used in a moment of distress, they can soften fear, interrupt shame, and return you to the heart of Grace. Keep them close. Write them in your journal, place them on your altar, tuck them into your passport.

You are not alone.

You are always welcome here.

Grace is never far. It lives in every breath, every return, every act of remembering.

The Grace Pledge

A Sacred Vow to Love Yourself Forward

You've opened your heart to the energy of Grace.

You've started listening inward; gently, honestly, soulfully.

Through five sacred questions, you've reconnected with the parts of you that have always known:

You are worthy of kindness.

You are worthy of respect.

You are allowed to soften.

You are deserving of tenderness.

You are someone worth staying with when life gets messy.

In asking the questions, you remember:

You matter.

You belong.

You are a vital part of the equation of life.

And still, there will be moments when you forget.

When doubt returns. When old stories rise.

When the fog sets in and you feel far from yourself.

That's why we pause here.

To make a vow.

Not to be perfect. Not to never fall.

But to stay with yourself, especially when it's hardest.

This is your Grace Pledge.

A personal declaration. A sacred promise to meet yourself with compassion instead of criticism, with tenderness, instead of toughness.

It's the reminder that Grace is not something you chase; it's something you choose.

Again. And again.

Especially in the quiet, private moments when no one else is watching.

Let this be your anchor when the storms roll in.

Your guiding light when the path feels unclear.

Your love letter to yourself. Written in courage, wrapped in reverence, sealed with compassion.

Create Your Grace Pledge

A Personal Vow of Self-Love, Wholeness & Devotion

Use the space below to write a pledge to yourself.

Let it be real.

Let it be yours.

Let it hold you in the days when grace feels far away.

There is no wrong way to do this; only your truth, spoken back to you in love.

Here are a few samples for inspiration:

Sample 1:

I vow to be soft with myself in moments of struggle.

I will not abandon my heart, even when it aches.

I promise to forgive myself, again and again, and to remember that healing is not linear.

I will walk gently, breathe deeply, and rest when I need to. I am no longer available for self-cruelty.

I choose Grace.

Sample 2:

I pledge to stand by my own side.

To speak kindly to myself, especially when the world feels loud and unkind.

I will honor my emotions, trust my intuition, and hold space for every version of me.

I vow to treat myself like someone I love.

From this day forward, I choose to live in alignment with Grace

Sample 3:

I promise to soften instead of strive, to listen instead of judge. When I fall, I will offer myself tenderness.

When I shine, I will allow it.

I release the pressure to perform, and I root into the truth that I am already enough.

My Grace is not earned. It is embodied.

Your Grace Pledge

A Fill-in-the-Blank Template for Self-Love, Wholeness & Devotion

I, _____,

choose to walk this journey with Grace.

I vow to meet myself with _____,

even when I feel _____.

I will honor my need for _____,

and offer myself _____ when I fall short.

I promise to return to _____

when I forget my worth.

I am worthy of _____,

and I choose to love myself through _____.

(Sign your name and date here)

Your Soul Star

From True North to the Soul Star: Aligning with the Divine Direction Within

Throughout this journey, we've spoken of *True North;* your inner compass, the quiet pull that guides you toward your most authentic self.

It isn't found on any map, but it lives inside your being, calibrated by truth, intuition, and the sacred language of the heart.

It's your internal direction-finder, aligned not by external expectations, but by inner wisdom.

But what if we zoomed out even further?

What if we looked not just at where you're going... but who is guiding you there?

In Qigong and energy medicine, there is a point known as the *Soul Star*—a luminous energy center located just above the crown of your head.

It is said to be the energetic gateway to your higher self, your soul path, and your divine blueprint.

It holds the knowing of who you truly are beneath the noise, beyond the roles, beyond the conditioning.

If your Inner Compass points toward your personal truth, the Soul Star is the celestial satellite that beams that truth down.

It is the transmitter of your soul's deepest direction; the origin of your True North.

When we feel lost, scattered, or disconnected, it's often because we've fallen out of alignment with this higher frequency of Grace.

This star is not something you have to create. It's already there, glowing just above you.

Your role is simply to remember it. To realign with it.

To reconnect with the radiance that has always been guiding you home.

Looking Ahead

Later in this book, you'll have an opportunity to be guided through a **Soul Star Activation;** a sacred ritual designed to help you align your body, your heart, and your higher self with the five elements of the heart of Grace.

For now, simply let the knowing of this star rest above you like a quiet beacon.

You don't need to reach for it.

Just remember...It's already yours.

A Special Note to You

Dear Beautiful Soul,

As we move forward on this journey, my intention for you is to take your time. There is no need to rush through the pages. No pressure to finish.

Allow yourself to sit with each chapter. Let the words meet you where you are, and the truths soak into your soul.

If something stirs, pause. If something aches, listen.

Whatever arises is not in your way. It *is* the way.

This is not just a book. It's an invitation to return; to your heart, to your wholeness.

So go gently. Be curious. Trust the timing of your own becoming.

You are worth every moment this journey takes.

PART II

THE HEART OF GRACE

"Your task is not to seek for love, but merely to seek and find all the barriers within yourself that you have built against it." — *Rumi*

GENTLENESS

"Gentleness is the Antidote for Cruelty."
— *Phaedrus*

There is a quiet kind of power in gentleness. Not the kind that shouts or forces, but the kind that softens and still heals. Gentleness isn't weakness. It's wisdom. It knows that real transformation happens not through pressure, but through presence. It offers grace without condition and love without performance. And for many women I work with, it's the one thing they give to everyone else but never themselves.

Gentleness is the first Element of Grace because it is the *gateway*. It opens the door to all the others. Without it, reverence becomes unreachable. Acceptance feels like failure. Compassion turns into obligation. Empathy becomes burnout. Gentleness is how we return to ourselves, and without it, we cannot truly receive anything. Not even love.

R*eceiving* is a key piece here. So many women have been conditioned to give endlessly, to meet everyone else's needs, to pour from a cup that was never filled. They show up in toxic relationships. They over-deliver. They protect others by abandoning themselves. Eventually, they become strangers to their own inner voice and needs. Their nervous systems are frayed, but their smiles stay intact.

They become hardened… not because they are unloving, but because they are *unheld.*

What Does It Mean to Be *Unheld*?

To be unheld is to move through life without your inner world being fully seen, heard, or tended to. It's not just about being unloved, it's about being unseen, unsupported, or unacknowledged in your truest self.

When you are unheld:

- Your *needs go quiet* because they've been ignored for too long.
- Your *heart grows cautious* because softness has not always been safe.
- You *over function* in relationships, workplaces, or families where you feel responsible for everyone else's wellbeing.

- You might not even know what you need anymore because your survival required you to disconnect from yourself.

Being unheld often begins in childhood, deepens in toxic or one-sided relationships, and gets reinforced by cultural narratives that glorify self-sacrifice. Especially for women. You're praised for being strong, for giving endlessly, for never complaining. But inside, you're withering, longing, and wondering why you're so tired all the time.

Over time this unheldness creates a hardness. Not because you are unloving, but because it's too painful to keep reaching into emptiness.

This is why *Gentleness* matters so much. It is the energy that starts to meet you where others have not. It allows you to begin receiving the care, the compassion, and the acknowledgment you've longed for. It's not something that comes from the outside, it begins with how you treat yourself.

Gentleness is how we begin to meet our own unmet and unheld needs and desires. It is the hand we extend to the parts of us that were left without the warmth of care or the soft space of understanding.

Let this chapter be the start of that meeting.

Let this be your return.

A Divine Message: "Put the U Back into Beautiful"

Several years ago, I received a message in a dream that changed my life. I was asleep, somewhere between the conscious and the unconscious, when a phrase kept repeating itself like a gentle drumbeat:

"Put the U back into beautiful…"

I tossed and turned to this mysterious phrase echoing in my mind. I prayed I would remember it in the morning. But when I woke, it was gone.

Later, while the water rushed over me in the shower, the message returned with a gentle force:

Put the U back into beautiful.

It didn't make sense, at least not right away. But something in me knew it was sacred. I stepped out, grabbed my journal, and wrote the word "beautiful" without the "U." Here's what I saw:

BEAT I FUL

In that moment, it hit me like lightning. I was being shown just how cruel I had become to myself. I wasn't just missing gentleness. I was actively beating myself up. For everything. I carried deep shame, unrealistic expectations, and the constant belief that I wasn't doing enough, being enough, giving enough.

It was a divine wake-up call. A whisper from Grace itself:

Stop the chaos.

Stop the inner cruelty.

Stop the self-abandonment.

Put YOU back into beautiful.

Because YOU are the missing piece.

Gentleness: The Gateway to Grace

Grace was calling me back to myself; not to hustle harder or fix more, but to soften. To open. To allow.

Gentleness is how we unlearn the inner punishment. It's how we let love in. It's how we come home. Without gentleness, we harden, we numb, we shut down. But when we let it in, when we practice it, Gentleness becomes the very frequency through which Grace flows.

Let me ask you something:

When was the last time you received or experienced true gentleness?

How are you relating to yourself right now?

Would you ever speak to a friend the way you speak to yourself?

If your best friend was hurting, would you berate her or would you offer her your presence, softness, understanding?

You deserve the same.

The Divine Feminine & the Power of Receiving

Gentleness is the essence of the Divine Feminine. She is not forceful. She does not coerce or demand. She receives. She nurtures. She allows. She listens.

To embody Gentleness is to say:

- *I do not have to earn love by over-giving.*
- *I can allow myself to receive.*
- *I am worthy of soft landings, quiet moments, and unconditional kindness.*

Receiving is a sacred act of opening. And opening requires safety. That safety begins with how we treat ourselves.

Gentleness in Balance vs. Out of Balance

Let's look at how Gentleness shows up, or goes missing, across three key areas of your life.

In Relationship with Yourself

In balance:

- You allow rest without guilt.
- You speak to yourself with kindness.
- You forgive your imperfections and celebrate your essence.

Out of balance:

- You push yourself beyond exhaustion.
- You criticize every flaw.
- You find it difficult to accept or receive love.

In Relationship with Others

In balance:

- You give without losing yourself.
- You speak your needs and set boundaries.
- You offer love from fullness, not depletion.

Out of balance:

- You people-please in order to keep peace.
- You silence yourself to avoid conflict.
- You carry responsibilities that don't belong to you.

In Relationship with the Divine

In balance:

- You feel unconditionally seen and loved.
- You trust that the Divine holds you with tenderness.
- You engage in spiritual practices that nourish rather than punish.

Out of balance:

- You believe love must be earned.
- You hide your pain in prayer.
- You feel unworthy of receiving Divine Grace— believing it's something to earn instead of something that already lives within you.

But Grace, in its truest form, is not distant or reserved for the deserving. It is the ever-present kindness of the Divine, waiting to be received.

A Gentle Invitation

As we close this chapter, I invite you to pause and breathe. Place your hand over your heart and whisper to yourself:

*"I am learning to treat myself with gentleness.
I am worthy of softness.*

I am worthy of Grace."

Let that be enough.

Let *you* be enough.

Reflective Exercise:

Close your eyes. Place your hand over your heart.

Ask,

"What part of me most needs gentleness right now?"

Then write from the voice of that part. Let her speak.

―――――――

Now that we have opened the gateway to Grace, the path ahead calls us to go deeper. Gentleness meets you at the door, but Reverence invites you to cross the threshold. Together, we'll explore what it means to not just offer yourself softness, but *sacred regard*. To see your own being as *inherently precious*, *worthy of honor*, and *deserving of your deepest devotion*.

REVERENCE

"You are not a drop in the ocean. You are the entire ocean in a drop." — Rumi

There is a kind of reverence that feels heavy, rigid, and formal. It's the kind many of us were taught in churches or traditions that framed God as distant and dangerous; something to bow before out of fear, not love. In those spaces, reverence meant silence, obedience, and self-erasure. You were told to diminish yourself to show respect for something greater.

But that's not the reverence we're exploring here.

The Reverence of Grace is not rooted in fear; it is rooted in remembrance. It is the sacred act of honoring yourself as worthy, whole, and divine. Not because of what you've done, but because of who you are. It's not about hierarchy. It's about wholeness. Not about worshiping something "out there," but recognizing the living presence of the Divine inside.

Imagine, just for a moment, what it would feel like to rise in the morning, look into your own eyes, and say:

"Good morning, Your Grace."

Not as flattery. Not as a performance. But as a sacred greeting; a bow to the sovereign soul within you. To the wisdom behind your eyes. To the beauty that cannot be diminished.

Reverence becomes a practice of crowning yourself with dignity; not because you seek to dominate, but because you're ready to take your rightful seat at the center of your life. It's not about making others small. It's about no longer shrinking yourself.

This is how we begin to embody the Grace that already lives within us; not through grandeur, but through groundedness. Not through perfection, but by showing up to life as we are, with an openhearted presence.

What is Presence?

Presence means being fully here with yourself; mind, body, heart, and soul, without the need to fix, flee, or perform. It's the quiet decision to meet your life with tenderness, to stop waiting until you're "better" to be worthy of love. Presence anchors you in grace because it brings you home to the truth of your being:

"I can be with myself, just as I am."

Reverence Is How You Return

Reverence is the energy that whispers:

"My feelings matter. My body is sacred. My boundaries are valid. My truth is worthy of honor."

It's not pride. It's remembrance. Not self-centeredness but soul-centeredness. Reverence reclaims your seat at the table, not by groveling, but by recognizing your preciousness.

It is how you return to yourself; your center, your truth, your inherent worth. It gently guides you back from the places you've drifted: self-abandonment, comparison, burnout, and the ache for outside approval. Reverence brings you home. It reminds you: you've never been broken, only disconnected.

Most women I know don't struggle with reverence because they're disrespectful but because they've been conditioned to prioritize everyone else. They've learned to bow outward and overlook inward. They offer honor generously but rarely give it back to themselves.

This chapter is an invitation to shift that.

To stand in the mirror of your own life and crown yourself; not with ego, but with essence. Not to elevate yourself above anyone but to finally rise and meet the sacredness that has always lived within you.

Because how can you offer reverence to life, to love, to God… if you're still rejecting the light inside yourself?

Why Reverence Matters in the Heart of Grace

Reverence is the sacred lens through which all other aspects of Grace come alive. Without it, Grace has nowhere to land. Self-love cannot take root in soil that does not honor the self.

Where Gentleness softens, Reverence remembers. It remembers that you are sacred. That your body is a vessel, not an afterthought. That your existence has value beyond performance or productivity. That the Divine isn't just above you, it lives within you.

Reverence is the golden thread that connects us to the sacredness of all life. It calls us to pause, to notice, to honor what often goes unseen. It's not simply respect; it's soul recognition. A deep bow to the mystery and meaning woven through every moment.

And it begins within.

To honor life, we must first honor ourselves. That means looking inward with eyes of love, not judgment. It means seeing our shadows not as enemies, but as teachers. When we approach them with reverence, we unlock the wisdom hidden inside and begin the journey toward wholeness.

Reverence then extends outward. It teaches us to see the sacred in others, even when they challenge us. It asks us to look through the eyes of the soul, not the lens of ego. From that space, we meet life with grace.

Reverence Transforms Your Inner Landscape

When you hold yourself with reverence, your story, your scars, your longings, and your voice become worthy of love. Reverence says:

"This is not just a life. This is a soul in motion."

It invites you to treat your healing as a sacred unfolding not a checklist of fixes. It shifts your posture from judgement to acceptance. From self-critique to self-blessing.

Reverence and Self-Love

Without reverence, self-love can stay surface level:

- Bubble baths without boundaries
- Mantras without meaning
- Affirmations without embodiment

But self-love infused with reverence becomes a living devotion. A sacred rhythm. A way of walking through the world with your head high; not in arrogance, but in alignment with your sacred worth.

You stop settling for crumbs. You stop shrinking your voice. You begin to speak, choose, rest, and rise as someone who knows:

I am not a drop in the ocean. I am the entire ocean in a drop.

Reverence In Balance & Out of Balance*Reverence in Relationship with Self*

In Balance:

- You honor your body, your truth, and your limits.
- You nourish yourself with love, not punishment.
- You listen inwardly. You set boundaries without guilt.
- You show up for yourself not from obligation, but devotion.
- Your inner voice is kind, firm, and rooted in self-worth.

Out of Balance:

- You override your needs and abandon your intuition.
- You push your body until it crashes.

- You second-guess your truth, silencing yourself to keep the peace.
- Your worth feels conditional based on how much you do, how well you perform, or how little space you take up.
- You silence your truth to avoid conflict.
- You forget your sacredness and settle for scraps.

Reverence in Relationship with Others

In Balance:

- You honor others without losing yourself.
- You respect differences while standing in your truth.
- You meet others with heart, not hierarchy.
- You bow to their journey while staying grounded in your own.

Out of Balance:

- You exalt others while dimming your own light.
- You confuse self-sacrifice with love.
- You stay small to make others comfortable.
- Reverence flows out, but not in; leaving your own needs unmet and your spirit overlooked.

Reverence in Relationship with the Divine

In Balance:

- You know the Divine as a living presence, not a distant judge.
- Your connection is tender, honest, and alive.
- You feel safe to question, to wrestle, to commune.
- Prayer becomes conversation. Ritual becomes relationship.
- Grace becomes the path beneath your feet.

Out of Balance:

- You approach the Divine through fear, shame or performance.
- You seek approval rather than connection.
- You silence your desires to appear more "holy."
- You feel unworthy of love because old beliefs told you so.

A Personal Story of Returning to Reverence

I shared this story in my essay published in *Shine Your Soul Light.* For some of you, this may be a repeat, but for others it will be a powerful example of what life can feel like when we live out of alignment with reverence.

After I left my marriage, I knew I needed time to heal; time to get my bearings. But I had no idea what that looked like. I read. I prayed. I listened. And I followed the guidance. In time, I was led to sign up for training in shadow work at the Ford Institute.

During that time, we did many guided meditations where I repeatedly visualized myself traveling into a long, deep, dark hole. I kept wondering why this image continued to appear. Eventually, I realized I was traveling into a well. I could see something at the bottom; a shape in a heap on the dank, muddy ground. But I always stopped short. Fear and resistance would rise, and I couldn't get close enough to see.

For months, this image returned. Each time, I inched closer. Finally, I got near enough to make out the silhouette of a person lying in a fetal position. Naked. Long, matted hair. Covered in dirt. I was shaken but somehow found the courage to approach and ask what she was doing there.

The woman lifted her twisted, emaciated body and slowly pushed her tangled hair from her face. With a faint whisper, she said, "Where have you been? Why have you forgotten me?"

Stunned and speechless, my life began flashing before my eyes.

Who was this? Why would she think I had forgotten her? My whole life had been about caring for others, trying to keep my marriage together, emotionally supporting my children, processing loss and fear. Who was I forgetting?

I looked closer and asked, "Who are you?"

We locked eyes. And in that instant, I knew. She was me.

As this awareness washed over me, the floodgates opened. All the pain and suffering I had buried came rushing forward. I had wanted to be loved so desperately that, for seventeen years, I had pretzeled myself to fit someone else's mold and expectations. I had lost who I was. When I wasn't terrified, I was numb. A shell of a woman who no longer recognized herself.

The soul of my being had been tossed to the bottom of a dark, empty well, waiting for me to come to her rescue. And in that moment, I realized: I had betrayed and abandoned myself long before the betrayal and abandonment in my marriage.

I leaned in and held her. We wept. I apologized and asked what she needed from me.

Her voice was soft, but her words were clear: "Don't ever leave me again."

So, I picked her up. I vowed to always be by her side. I washed her, clothed her, and placed a crown on her head. Together, we began the deep process of healing through loving-kindness, grace, and the care she had needed for a very long time.

That moment was the beginning of a new way of living; a sacred vow not just to care for others, but to revere myself as well. I had been searching for Grace, only to realize it was waiting for me at the bottom of the well. And it wasn't in the form of perfection, or approval, or performance. It was in the simple act of returning to myself with tenderness, devotion, and truth.

Every day since has been a practice in keeping that vow. And one of the most powerful tools I've found to continue honoring it... is the mirror.

Mirror of Alignment: A Reverence Ritual

There is a sacred power in seeing yourself clearly and honoring what you see. Reverence invites us to turn toward our own reflection; not to critique, but to connect.

Each morning, try this simple ritual:

1. Stand before a mirror. Let your gaze soften.
2. Place your hand gently over your heart.
3. Take a slow, conscious breath.
4. Look into your own eyes and say: *"Good morning, Your Grace."*

Let it be more than a greeting. Let it be a homecoming. A

sacred pause. A moment of reunion with your own divinity.

This is not about flattery or performance. It is about connecting to the essence of you. You are meeting the divine spark within you with honor and affection. Over time, this sacred pause becomes a thread that weaves reverence into the fabric of your daily life.

You are not a mistake to fix.

You are a mystery to honor.

And every time you bow to the truth of your sacredness, you return to the heart of Grace.

Reflections - Journal Prompts

- Where am I not honoring myself right now?
- Where have I mistaken self-sacrifice for love?
- What beliefs have shaped my relationship with the Divine, and are they aligned with grace?

A Final Word on Reverence

Reverence is not a one-time act. It's a way of being. A sacred posture you choose again and again, even when it's hard. Especially when it's hard.

Every time you meet your reflection with kindness...

Every time you speak your truth without shrinking...

Every time you honor your needs without apology...

You are practicing Reverence. You are embodying Grace.

And you are returning to the sacred center that has never left you.

As we leave the sanctuary of Reverence, we prepare to enter the next sacred element of Grace:

Acceptance. The gentle art of letting go of resistance and welcoming all parts of who we are.

ACCEPTANCE

*"The curious paradox is that when I accept myself just as
I am, then I can change." – Carl Rogers*

A cceptance is the act of seeing yourself clearly and choosing to love what you see.

It's not resignation. It's not apathy. It's a deep breath that says:

"I am enough, even as I grow."

Acceptance is the stabilizing, grounding element of self-love.

It's the part that says, "It is what it is," not with flippancy or defeat, but with calm assurance.

It anchors us in the present moment and reminds us:

All is well. Just as it is. Just as you are.

From this grounded space, we regulate.

Our nervous system begins to settle.

The frantic search for approval slows.

We stop performing and start *being*.

Acceptance opens the door to healing.

It softens the inner critic, dissolves shame, and gives us permission to be messy, magnificent, and in-progress.

It creates a sacred neutrality from which clarity and aligned choices can emerge.

It reminds us:

"You don't have to earn love by becoming someone else. You already are someone worth loving."

It's the steady space where striving subsides, and something new starts to take root.

Why Acceptance is Essential to Grace

Without Acceptance, Grace cannot take root.

It needs more than an idea or a belief, it needs a place to live.

Grace flows into the places within us that feel safe enough to receive it. That safety grows when we stop pushing ourselves away and begin honoring the fullness of who we've always been.

When we're caught in self-rejection, Grace hovers like a bird with no branch to rest on.

But when we begin to accept ourselves, even in our messiness, Grace settles in.

It becomes a steady presence, not just something we reach for in crisis.

Acceptance prepares the inner soil.

If Gentleness opens the heart, and Reverence bows to the sacredness of our being, then Acceptance is the grounded knowing that says:

"You belong...right here, right now...just as you are."

Only from this rooted place can we receive the fullness of Grace; not as a reward to be earned, but as a birthright to be remembered.

A Personal Journal Entry from the In-Between

When I began writing this book, I knew I would be walking alongside you not ahead. I've come to see this project not just as something I'm creating, but something that's creating me.

Acceptance doesn't happen in theory. It happens in the moments we're willing to meet ourselves right in the thick of it.

Here's one of those moments for me...

February 27

Dear T.O. (I address my entries to "Treasured One")

I have been working on collecting ideas for my book and the journey I want to take the readers on. Journey to the Heart of Grace... what is this exactly?

I feel like I can get down deep into the weeds but also want to keep it more simple.

Yet, I am compelled to dive into the space somewhere in between.

I am chuckling because I feel like I live my life in the in-between space—the space that moves me from the past into the future.

How interesting that as we move from that space, we aren't where we were, and we haven't arrived at where we want to go.

Ironically, this space could be called the space that is happening NOW.

The present time we find ourselves in.

I used to feel stuck here until this epiphany: the in-between space is the space of now.

So much happens here, and at the same time when we aren't moving fast, or as fast as we want to go, we feel stuck.

We feel like there is something wrong with us.

We compare ourselves to others and wonder why it may seem so easy for them but difficult for ourselves.

I have felt like I have perpetually been in the space of "in-between;" working out kinks, patterns, and healing junk that has gotten in the way of what feels like moving forward.

What I fail to recognize at times, is this is the space of fertile ground.

So much happens in this space that isn't seen externally, but it's the inner growth, healing, and seeding of the future.

It's where the transformation happens.

It is also where time collapses.

Where the past meets the present, and the present touches the future.

If we are constantly growing and stepping into newer, truer versions of ourselves, we will always carry the in-between with us.

Reflection

This journal entry was a turning point—a gentle moment of clarity where I began to recognize the wisdom in my own timing.

If you read between the lines, you can feel the beginning of *self-acceptance* taking form.

It showed me how I had been hard on myself. How self-judgment had become a way of holding myself back, of staying small.

But through writing and meeting myself where I was, I began to release that grip.

The resistance started to shift, and I was finally able to embrace the process; the truth of what was.

From this place, possibility began to take shape.

And I realized: things are okay.

I am okay.

This is the sacred invitation of Acceptance.

Not to arrive, but to allow.

To allow the unfolding.

To claim the messy middle as *holy ground.*

The Space In-between

Acceptance is the still space between breaths.

The soft moment between letting go and what comes next.

It is the open field where nothing is forced, and everything belongs.

Acceptance In Balance & Out of Balance

Acceptance in Relationship to Self

In Balance:

- Acceptance is a fierce kind of love.
- It doesn't ignore our flaws; it includes them. It says, *"Even here, you are worthy."*
- It stabilizes the inner landscape so that growth can come from love, not lack.

Out of Balance:

- Self-rejection masquerades as self-improvement.
- We chase an ideal, believing we are only lovable *once we arrive.*
- We judge, withhold compassion, and deny our imperfections.

Acceptance in Relationships with Others

In Balance:

- Acceptance in relationships offers freedom.
- It allows others to be who they are and grants us the same permission.
- We communicate honestly, honor differences, and meet each other with respect instead of resistance.

Out of Balance:

- When acceptance is missing, we try to fix, change, or control others; or we shapeshift ourselves to gain love.
- Relationships feel conditional, reactive, or filled with hidden expectations.
- We become performers rather than participants.

Acceptance in Relationship with the Divine

In Balance:

- True acceptance of self opens the doorway to intimate connection with the Divine.
- There's no longer a need to pretend.
- We realize we are already loved, already worthy, already included in the embrace of the Divine.

Out of Balance:

- Many of us inherited spiritual beliefs that linked love to performance.
- We believed we had to earn grace, act holy, or hide our broken parts to stay connected to God.
- This creates spiritual disconnection and shame.

Reflections – Journal Prompts

- What part of myself have I been resisting, avoiding, or rejecting?
- Where am I trying to fix something that might actually need to be accepted first?
- How would I treat myself if I truly believed *I am already enough*?
- Can I pause in this moment and say to myself: "It is what it is. And all is well"?

The Grounding Ritual of Acceptance

Place both feet flat on the ground.

Place your hands over your heart.

Close your eyes and breathe.

Let your breath move slowly in and out.

Feel the floor beneath you.

Say softly:

> *"I am here. I am whole.*
> *I accept myself just as I am.*
> *All is well."*

Repeat as often as needed; especially when doubt, shame, or self-criticism arise. Let this practice become your anchor.

Stepping Into Compassion

Acceptance is where the soil softens.

Where resistance yields.

Where truth is no longer something to fight, but something to hold.

And yet, there are moments when seeing ourselves clearly still stings. Even after we've grounded into "what is," we may still carry judgment, fear, or sorrow. This is where the next element of Grace enters—Compassion.

Compassion begins the moment we stop resisting our pain and choose to meet it with gentleness.

It is the balm that soothes what Acceptance reveals.

It holds the trembling parts of us with tenderness and says:

"Even this… even you… are worthy of love."

In the next chapter, we will explore what it means to offer that kind of kindness to ourselves and how, from that place, we become capable of extending it to others in a way that is real, rooted, and whole.

Let's journey on into the heart of Compassion.

COMPASSION

"Compassion is not a soft sentiment. It is fierce tenderness—the kind that holds space for healing without judgment."— *Inspired by Rumi*

This morning, as I sat preparing to write this chapter, I pulled a card from one of my oracle decks.

It read: *Healing the Heart — the Power of Self-Love.*

How appropriate. How necessary.

Because I realize we cannot talk about Compassion without first acknowledging heartbreak.

Over the course of a lifetime, our hearts will break in countless ways:

- The loss of a child
- The death of a spouse
- Divorce
- Broken relationships
- Betrayal
- Abuse
- Rejection
- Abandonment
- Unfulfilled dreams

Each of these experiences can cause us to grieve, to mourn, to withdraw.

We shut down. We push through. We survive—but at a cost.

We turn to coping mechanisms because feeling everything at once is too much.

We stop trusting—not just others, but ourselves.

We wonder if we're even worthy of love at all.

And yet... beneath all that hurt, there is a tender longing:

A desire to be held. To be seen. To be safe.

To feel again. To love again. To trust again.

This is where Compassion enters—

Not as a solution, but as a sanctuary.

What Is Compassion?

Compassion is the heartfelt desire to ease suffering—both our own and others'.

It arises when we *recognize* pain, feel moved by it, and feel compelled to respond with care, kindness, or supportive action.

It isn't just about noticing or understanding someone's pain; It's about stepping toward it with love.

At its core, compassion holds this message:

> *"I see your pain, and I want to help ease it. I want to bring care where there is suffering."*

Compassion has warmth, intention, and *movement.*

It's not just a feeling—it's also a response.

It lives in the heart *and* in the hands.

It shows up in quiet moments:

- When we choose to stay with our pain instead of turning away.
- When we offer a kind word to ourselves instead of harsh judgment.
- When we sit with someone else's suffering and simply say, *"I'm here."*

It is both a balm and a bridge.

A sacred force that reminds us: *You don't have to carry this alone.*

Compassion is not pity.

It is not weakness.

It is a fierce and gentle form of grace.

The act of wrapping ourselves in loving-kindness when we are most undone.

It's the courage to meet ourselves in the messy, broken places with tenderness instead of judgment.

Compassion creates a safe space for vulnerability, for honesty, and for healing.

Until we can name *what really broke our hearts*, we cannot truly heal.

Compassion invites us to speak those truths aloud—to ourselves first.

It says:

> *"You can fall apart here. I won't leave you."*

When we learn to hold ourselves in that space, we begin to understand our own strength.

We don't have to perform.

We don't have to be perfect.

We just have to *be present* with ourselves - as we are.

Why Compassion is Essential to Grace

Without Compassion, Grace has no way to move through pain.

Compassion is what allows Grace to reach the wounded places in us without judgment, without rush.

It is the gentle companion that walks with us through grief, heartbreak, and shame—not to fix or erase them, but to *honor* them.

Where Acceptance says, *"This is what is,"*

Compassion adds, *"And I will stay with you through it."*

Compassion makes Grace personal.

It's the expression of Grace that holds your hand when everything else falls away.

It's what softens the walls around your heart so healing can enter.

It allows you to be *with* your pain without being consumed by it.

Without Compassion, Grace risks becoming conceptual —something we talk about but never truly *feel*.

But when Compassion is present, Grace becomes touchable.

It breathes. It weeps. It holds.

Compassion is what transforms Grace from an idea into a sanctuary.

A Personal Turning Point

A few years ago, I was deeply grieving.

I was still healing from my divorce, had recently lost my father, remarried, and was trying to navigate the complexities of blending families.

On the outside, I was building a new life.

But on the inside, I was carrying so much loss.

More than I had even allowed myself to name.

My heart was broken. But I didn't really realize it at the time.

I was pushing forward. Performing. Surviving.

I knew there was some unresolved grief around my

father's passing, but I had no idea how much pain I was actually carrying—until one night, I broke.

I went to bed but couldn't sleep.

Tears started to flow.

It was late, and I didn't want to wake my new husband.

To be honest, I didn't want him to *know* I was crying.

I couldn't receive love or comfort from anyone.

My whole life had been dedicated to supporting others; being the caretaker, the strong one, the emotional rock.

I had buried what was happening in my own emotional world. Everything felt so incredibly heavy.

And then, somewhere in the quiet of those early morning hours, I met myself.

Not the version I showed to the world.

But the real me: the exhausted, heartbroken, deeply feeling *me.*

My higher self—my wise adult—stepped in.

She held space for the broken little girl inside of me.

She didn't try to fix her. She just *held her.*

And in doing so, I began to witness the timeline of my life... Twenty-plus years of carrying, helping, hiding, enduring.

I cried for hours. I felt like a mess.

A *beautiful* mess.

I was finally being met with the love and compassion I so desperately needed.

At some point, I got out of bed, wrapped myself in a blanket, grabbed my journal, and poured everything out onto the page.

My adult self-stayed with me the whole time, holding me until the very last tear fell.

That night marked a turning point in my healing.

I learned that I could be there for myself.

I could be raw and vulnerable and *safe* in my own presence.

I didn't need to look outside of myself for love and affirmation—I had it within me all along.

I'm still learning how to open up and receive from others.

But that night showed me the power of self-compassion.

And it changed everything.

Compassion in Relationship with Self – The Sacred Return

Compassion begins at home within the sacred space of your own heart.

When we offer ourselves compassion, we stop demanding perfection and start honoring our pain.

We allow ourselves to feel what we feel without shame.

We cradle our grief, our fear, our overwhelm—just as we would comfort a child waking from a nightmare.

This is the moment when we become our own safe place.

Self-compassion doesn't mean we excuse harmful behavior or avoid growth.

It's not self-indulgence—it's *truth*.

It asks us to look honestly at what's happening beneath the surface and respond with care, not criticism.

When we can say to ourselves, "I see you. I know this is hard. And I am here," we begin to heal.

This is the foundation of all other compassion.

Without it, we often give to others what we deny ourselves—and over time, that imbalance hollows us out.

True compassion with self is not a luxury.

It's a lifeline.

Compassion in Relationship with Others – The Gift of Presence

Compassion with others means we meet people where they are—not where we wish they were.

It's the ability to hold space for another's pain without needing to fix it, change it, or carry it for them.

It's listening without judgment.

Being present without performance.

Loving without control.

But here's where it gets blurry.

We often confuse compassion with codependency—especially if we've spent years being the strong one, the helper, or the emotional glue in our relationships.

Codependency is not love.

It's self-abandonment dressed in concern.

It's when our sense of worth becomes entangled with another person's well-being.

We lose our center because we're so busy managing theirs.

Compassion vs. Codependency

Compassion	Co-dependency
"I care about you'	"I need to fix you to feel okay"
Holds space with love and limits	Absorbs the other's pain and neglects the self
Respects the others path	Tries to control or rescue them
Is rooted in wholeness	Is driven by fear, guilt, or unment needs

Compassion says:

"I'm here with you, and I trust you can find your way."

Codependency says:

"Let me carry you—because if you fall, I will too."

One is a posture of grace.

The other, a survival strategy we learned when our own needs were ignored.

When we start offering ourselves compassion, we unhook from the need to *prove* our love through sacrifice.

We stop bleeding for others to feel needed.

Instead, we begin loving from a place of *overflow* rather than depletion.

This is the holy shift from *self-abandonment* to *self-honoring*—and it's where true compassion begins to flourish.

For those who have spent a lifetime believing that love must come at the cost of themselves, this is a clarifying and liberating invitation: to love without losing yourself.

Compassion in Relationship with The Divine – Reclaiming the Divine Embrace

Perhaps the hardest, and holiest, place to receive compassion is from the Divine.

For many of us, especially those healing from toxic spiritual teachings, the idea of a compassionate Source feels foreign.

We may have been taught to fear God rather than feel held by God.

To shrink in shame rather than rise in love.

But Grace tells a different story.

The compassion of Source is not earned—it is intrinsic.

It's not something you have to chase, prove, or deserve.

It is already within you—built in, like the warmth of sunlight or the rhythm of your heartbeat.

Divine compassion is part of your nature.

It flows from the very essence of Grace.

You don't have to reach a certain level of healing to receive it.

You don't have to have it all together.

You only need to remember—it's already yours.

It's not based on your behavior.

It's based on your being.

You are already worthy.

Already loved.

Already enough.

When we allow ourselves to soften into this truth, we begin to rebuild our trust in something greater.

Not as a force to fear, but as a presence that whispers:

"I see your wounds, and I call them sacred."

This kind of compassion restores our sense of belonging...

- To ourselves
- To each other
- And to the heart of Grace

Compassion out of Balance - When Care Hurts

Compassion is a force of love.

But like all sacred qualities, when it becomes distorted, withheld, or misunderstood, it no longer heals—it *hurts*.

When we offer too little compassion, too much compassion without boundaries, or perform it to gain approval, we move out of alignment with Grace.

These imbalances often arise not from a lack of love—but from unhealed wounds.

Too Little Compassion: The Cold Hearted

When we are disconnected from compassion—especially toward ourselves—we can become harsh, rigid, or self-punishing.

We hold ourselves to impossible standards.

Dismiss our needs.

Criticize our pain.

Instead of offering comfort, we offer judgment.

Instead of softness, we armor up.

This inner coldness makes it hard to receive love from anyone—including the Divine.

We don't trust it.

We don't believe we deserve it.

Too Much Compassion (Unboundaried): The Martyr Mask

When we give compassion without limits—especially to others—we risk crossing into *enabling, resentment,* or *emotional exhaustion.*

We take on pain that isn't ours.

Say yes when our bodies whisper no.

Abandon ourselves in the name of "being loving."

But martyrdom is not Grace.

Compassion without boundaries is not a gift. It's a slow erosion of the self.

It leaves us exhausted and disconnected from our own needs.

Performative Compassion: The Approval Trap

Sometimes, what we call compassion is really a performance for validation.

We help because we want to feel needed.

We show up because we're afraid of being rejected.

We offer care as currency for love.

This isn't true compassion. It's a transaction.

Unfortunately, some of us have learned this as a coping mechanism in unsafe environments.

It leaves us feeling empty.

Because no matter how much we give, it never fills the void inside.

The Return to Balance

Real compassion begins with honesty:

- What do I feel?
- What do I need?
- What can I offer, and what can I not?

When we recognize the places we've distorted compassion; either by withholding it, overextending it, or performing it—we can gently guide ourselves back to center.

Back to balance.

Back to grace.

The Golden-Stitched Heart – A Visual Metaphor for Compassion

There is an ancient Japanese art form called *Kintsugi*, where broken pottery is repaired using lacquer mixed with gold. The cracks are not hidden. They are illuminated. The break becomes part of the beauty.

This tradition inspired me to imagine something similar within us.

What if our hearts, after heartbreak, loss, and pain, could be mended not with shame or silence, but with something radiant?

What if our Compassion was the gold?

Imagine your heart as a sacred vessel; delicate, powerful, and alive with emotion.

Over the course of your life, this heart has cracked.

From grief.

From betrayal.

From rejection, loss, and longing.

But you didn't discard the pieces.

You began to gather them.

Gently. Slowly. Tenderly.

And with the energy of self-love and compassion, you began to stitch your heart back together; not with thread, but with gold.

Each crack became a place of light.

A place of wisdom.

A visible reminder: *This happened. And still, I am whole.*

Compassion doesn't erase the past.

It honors it.

It turns your heart into a masterpiece of healing.

Your scars are sacred seams.

Your healing is an art form.

You are not less because you were broken.

You are more because you chose to heal.

Reflection Exercise: The Golden-Stitched Heart

Find a quiet space. Light a candle if you feel called. Let this be a moment just for you.

Take a few deep breaths.

Place one hand on your heart, and one on your belly.

Close your eyes and begin to gently ground yourself in the present moment.

Visualize your heart—not as it "should" be, but as it *truly is.*

See its unique shape, its worn edges, the cracks it carries.

See the places where it has broken... and the places where it is

still soft, still tender.

Now imagine each of those cracks has been lovingly repaired; not hidden but highlighted with radiant golden seams.

Like a masterpiece of Kintsugi, your heart has been stitched together with compassion, wisdom, and grace.

As you hold this image, ask yourself:

- *Where have I broken open and begun to heal?*
- *What losses or heartbreaks have shaped the gold in me?*
- *What part of me still longs to be held with compassion?*
- *Where am I ready to forgive myself; for surviving the only way I knew how?*

Breathe into your answers. Let them rise from within, without judgment.

When you feel ready, open your journal and respond to this prompt:

Draw or describe your "Golden-Stitched Heart."

- *What stories do its seams tell?*
- *What makes it beautiful, just as it is?*

You may wish to sketch your heart on the page, letting your intuition guide the image.

Or simply write a love letter to the heart that has carried you through it all.

Closing Blessing: A Prayer of Compassion

May you be gentle with the parts of you still learning to breathe.

May you wrap yourself in tenderness where the ache still lingers.

May every crack in your heart become a golden invitation to Grace.

May you trust that you are not broken; you are becoming.

And may compassion meet you like warm hands in the dark, whispering:

> *"You are safe here. You are seen. You are already enough."*

From Compassion to Empathy: A Bridge of Connection

As we close this chapter on Compassion, may you carry its tenderness with you; a quiet reminder that love begins within, and that healing is an act of grace.

Yet compassion does not live in isolation.

It walks alongside another sacred companion on the path of grace: Empathy.

If Compassion is the soft place we land when we are hurting, then Empathy is the bridge that allows us to *feel with others;* to cross into their experience without losing our own.

Through Empathy we begin to understand not just our own pain, but the shared humanity that connects us all.

In the next chapter, we will explore what it means to feel deeply,

to attune to others without absorbing them,

and to remain anchored in ourselves while holding space for someone else.

We will also uncover the shadow side of empathy; when feeling too much becomes overwhelming and how to transform that sensitivity into strength, clarity, and presence.

You are ready.

Let us continue the journey,

heart open, feet steady.

Let us walk the bridge to Empathy—together.

EMPATHY

"Empathy is the medicine the world needs."
— Judith Orloff

E mpathy is the ability to share and understand the feelings of another.

It is the energy that creates safety, connection, and understanding in relationships. It allows us to step outside of our own perspective and into someone else's world; to not just *see* what they see, but to *feel* what they feel.

Empathy is more than a feeling. It's a presence.

It is the tender art of feeling with—not fixing, not absorbing, and not bypassing.

It is the grace of standing beside someone, including yourself, and saying with full awareness:

"I see you. I feel this with you. You are not alone."

More than sympathy. More than understanding.

Empathy is an embodied connection.

It lives in the heart, travels through the nervous system, and awakens our shared humanity.

It is a quiet attunement to another's inner experience.

It heightens our attention, expands our compassion, and challenges us to stretch our knowing beyond what is comfortable or familiar.

Empathy is a bridge linking heart to heart, experience to experience.

It weaves threads of belonging across our differences.

And when practiced with healthy boundaries, it allows us to walk beside others without losing ourselves.

Empathy holds space.

It listens without fixing.

It honors without judgment.

It says, *"Your experience matters."*

To walk in grace is to walk with empathy—

for others, for the world, and most especially for ourselves.

I believe Empathy is the medicine our world so desperately needs. Can you feel it? Can you imagine what might shift personally, culturally, globally if Empathy coursed through the veins of all of us?

Empathy: The Living Thread of Grace

Empathy heals what disconnection harms.

It mends the emotional ruptures we carry from childhood, culture, and even religion.

It reminds us that we are not broken; just *unseen* or *unheard* for too long.

Without empathy, wounds deepen in silence. But with empathy, healing begins; softly at first, then with strength.

Empathy builds bridges:

- Between the inner child and the adult self.
- Between partners, friends, and family.
- Between self-judgment and self-forgiveness.
- Between trauma and transformation.

When we are met with empathy, something sacred happens:

- *The nervous system exhales.*
- *The heart opens.*
- *The soul speaks.*

This is why Empathy is not just helpful, but it is essential to Grace.

Grace is the atmosphere in which healing happens.

Empathy is the *oxygen* within that atmosphere.

Without empathy, grace becomes a concept.

With empathy, grace becomes *a felt experience;* one that softens shame, quiets fear and invites us back into belonging.

Empathy is also how we embody grace in action.

It is how we extend the sacred back to ourselves and others in real-time moments of:

- Holding space for grief without rushing it.
- Listening deeply when someone shares their truth.
- Sitting with our own pain, without numbing or self-rejection.
- Offering kindness to the part of ourselves that still feels unworthy.

To live in grace is to live with an open heart.

Empathy is the gentle hand that keeps that heart open — even when it wants to close.

What Disconnect Looks Like

To understand the sacred power of Empathy, we must also witness what rises in its absence.

When empathy is missing, we often encounter:

- Apathy – the absence of care or feeling. Numbness.
- Indifference – a detachment that says, "Your experience doesn't matter to me."
- Cruelty or antipathy – where pain is not only ignored but sometimes mocked or intentionally inflicted.

Without empathy, emotional connection becomes nearly impossible.

Without empathy, suffering is overlooked.

Without empathy, people become objects, and relationships lose their soul.

Can you imagine a world without empathy?

I can...

And it's *not* a world I'd want to live in.

Empathy in Relationships

Empathy in Relationship to Self

In Balance: Presence with Ourselves

Empathy with ourselves is the practice of *feeling with* our inner experience; not judging it, rushing it, or explaining it away. It's when we tune in to our own emotional landscape with tenderness and curiosity. We ask ourselves: *What am I feeling? What do I need right now?* And we listen without shame.

When empathy is in balance, we offer ourselves the same presence we so often give others. We give ourselves permission to *be human*—to grieve, to stumble, to feel deeply without needing to be fixed.

It is an act of self-honoring that says:

"I will not abandon myself in this moment. I am here with you."

Out of Balance: Disconnection or Flooding

When empathy is missing in our relationship with ourselves, we become emotionally disconnected. We may numb out, silence our feelings, or override our intuition. We become the critic, the fixer, the performer—anything but present.

On the other hand, if we are overwhelmed by our own emotions without any grounding, empathy can turn into *emotional flooding.* We get lost in the waves without an anchor. Compassion helps regulate this by adding care and containment.

Without balanced self-empathy, we either avoid ourselves or drown in ourselves.

Empathy in Relationship with Others

In Balance: Attunement with Boundaries

Empathy with others is the ability to attune to someone else's emotional state while staying rooted in our own. It's the presence that says:

"I may not have experienced exactly what you're going through, but I'm here. I feel with you. You don't have to carry this alone."

Balanced empathy allows us to connect deeply *without absorbing* another person's pain. We witness, hold space, and offer our presence without trying to fix, rescue, or take responsibility for their emotions.

It honors both our emotional boundaries and theirs.

Out of Balance: Enmeshment or Emotional Avoidance

When empathy is out of balance with others, it can turn into *empathic enmeshment*—we feel everything so intensely that we lose sight of where we end and the other begins. Many highly sensitive people fall into this pattern unconsciously.

This is where empathy without boundaries becomes *exhausting*. We absorb pain that isn't ours. We feel responsible for others' happiness. We get emotionally drained, resentful, or overwhelmed.

On the flip side, when empathy is shut down, we may become cold, dismissive, or avoidant—unable or unwilling to feel what another is experiencing.

Empathy in balance is a sacred dance between *attunement* and *autonomy*.

Empathy in Relationship to the Divine

In Balance: The Sacred Mirror

Empathy with the Divine is the deep inner knowing that we are not alone in our experience. That there is a sacred presence that *feels with us*, weeps with us, celebrates with us.

It's the sense that the Divine is not distant or detached, but intimately aware of what it means to be human.

Empathy in this relationship sounds like:

"I am with you in this. You are not forgotten."

It brings comfort in pain, reassurance in silence, and strength in uncertainty.

Out of Balance: Feeling Abandoned or Unseen

When empathy with Source is absent or distorted, we may feel abandoned by the Divine. We may believe our suffering is unnoticed—or worse, deserved.

This often stems from toxic spiritual teachings that frame God as punitive, cold, or emotionally detached. It becomes difficult to trust that we are seen, heard, and deeply understood.

In this space, prayer can feel empty. Spiritual connection can feel unreachable.

But when we begin to imagine a God who weeps with us, who sits beside us in silence, who holds our pain in Their own heart, *healing begins.*

When Empathy Becomes Imbalanced – The Shadow Side

Empathy, when embodied with awareness, is one of the most beautiful expressions of grace.

But when it goes unchecked or unbalanced, it can quietly morph into exhaustion, entanglement, and even self-abandonment.

Many of the women I work with don't struggle because they lack empathy. They struggle because they have *too much empathy* and no boundaries to hold it.

Here are three common expressions of empathy in shadow:

1. The Over-Absorber: "I Feel Everything"

This is empathy without a filter.

You walk into a room and immediately feel what everyone else is carrying. You can't tell where *you* end, and *they* begin. You absorb other people's grief, anger, confusion, and anxiety—sometimes before they even speak it aloud.

Over time, this creates burnout, emotional overwhelm, and deep fatigue. Your system becomes flooded, and it becomes difficult to access your own needs or truth.

This kind of empathic entanglement often comes from childhood conditioning: when you were responsible for other people's emotions or learned that feeling deeply was the only way to stay safe or loved.

2. The Fixer or Savior: "It's My Job to Help"

In this pattern, empathy becomes fused with over-responsibility.

You feel someone's pain and then immediately feel the urge to *do something* about it. You become the emotional firefighter, always rushing in to put out flames.

But here's the truth: not all pain is yours to carry.

Not all wounds are yours to heal.

And sometimes, your desire to fix comes from a discomfort with sitting in the mess—not a true call to action.

Empathy in shadow can convince us that love means *saving* someone.

But grace says love means *being with* someone—without losing yourself in the process.

3. The Numb One: "I Can't Feel Anything"

On the flip side, some people experience the shadow of empathy not as over-feeling but as emotional numbness. This often arises after years of emotional burnout, trauma, or overwhelm.

When you've carried too much for too long, your system may begin to shut down. You stop feeling—not because you don't care, but because it's too painful to care. This kind of apathy is a survival mechanism, not a character flaw.

The invitation here is not to force empathy but to gently rebuild your capacity to feel in a way that honors your safety and sovereignty.

The Gift and the Cost of Sensitivity

Empathy is a sacred bridge; one that connects us to others, to the Divine, and to the tender truths within ourselves. But for those of us who feel deeply, especially the highly sensitive among us, this bridge can sometimes become blurred. Boundaries dissolve, emotional burdens accumulate, and we begin to lose our sense of center.

In my own life, empathy has been both a gift and a challenge. What began as a natural ability to feel with others eventually became a path to burnout, depletion, and emotional overwhelm. It wasn't until I began to understand the *energetics* of empathy—and reclaim my own sovereignty—that I found a new way forward.

What follows is a personal story about what it means to be a highly sensitive person in a world that doesn't always understand that gift... and how I learned to protect my own energy without losing my capacity to care.

My Journey as a Highly Sensitive Empath

I thought empathy would be the easiest chapter to write...

After all, I've spent the majority of my life tapped into other people's energy fields. I could sense what they were feeling, know how they felt, and often feel it in my own body. For years, I didn't understand what was happening. I didn't know it was different. I thought everyone felt this way.

Looking back, I believe it was both a gift I was born with *and* a survival tool I developed.

It came with a deep inner knowing. And while that ability has helped me support others in profound ways—it also nearly depleted me.

Later in life, I learned I was highly empathic. Some people called me an "Empath"—someone who sees, senses, and feels deeply. It was described as an intuitive gift. And it is. But like most gifts, it came with a cost.

My energy field would merge with others. I would *feel them*—in my mind, my body, my nervous system. This created a powerful sense of connection… and a powerful sense of obligation. I felt responsible. I felt compelled to reach out, to fix, to hold. I genuinely cared. But over time, I noticed how little energy I had left for myself.

The burnout was real.

So real, in fact, that I stepped away from coaching altogether. I started a business in a completely different field and stayed there for four years. And yet, even there, I found myself supporting the healing journey of my business partner, who was also highly sensitive. I realized: *I can't outrun what I'm called to do. I'm here to help people heal.* But I needed a new way to do it; one that included me.

The Hidden Roots of Sensitivity

Over time, I began to understand that not everyone who is highly sensitive is born that way.

Some of us become highly attuned as a way to survive.

When you live in a toxic environment, being hyper-aware can feel like safety.

You learn to read the room. You learn to feel shifts before they happen.

You learn to shape-shift, accommodate, and over-function… all in the name of peace.

I had lived this way for years—caring deeply, staying too long, trying to fix or save.

At some point, I had to ask myself: *But what about me?*

I was exhausted. Disconnected from my own needs.

I didn't know what I wanted anymore. I just knew I was tired. All. The. Time.

Even worse, I had fallen into patterns of *over-responsibility.*

I would take on extra work—not because the other person couldn't do it, but because I didn't want to deal with their emotional reactivity. It became easier to carry the burden myself.

But in doing so, I had completely abandoned *me.*

What I didn't know at the time was that I was bleeding energy.

Not just giving it out; I was absorbing it as well. Merging energy with others and holding what wasn't mine.

One of the most life-changing tools I learned was this simple question:

Whose energy is this? Theirs or mine?

If it was mine, I grounded myself.

I journaled. I tuned in. I listened with presence and care.

But if it was *theirs,* I learned to say, *"This is not mine."*

I would notice where I felt it in my body. Then, I'd visualize that energy moving—down through my body, through my legs, and out through my feet into the earth to be recycled.

- I began to reclaim my boundaries.
- I began to protect my nervous system.
- I began to come home to myself.

What I Know Now

Empathy is sacred but without boundaries, it becomes self-erasure.

Being highly sensitive is a gift but not one meant to drain us.

I now understand that my people-pleasing, my emotional over-responsibility, and my exhaustion were not flaws.

They were coping mechanisms. Strategies I learned in toxic spaces to keep the peace. To stay safe. To survive.

But I'm not surviving anymore. I'm learning to live— and live well.

I don't need to absorb the pain of others to show that I care.

I don't need to be the fixer to be valuable.

I can feel deeply and still be sovereign.

I can hold space for others while also holding space for *me.*

This is where I had to heal.

I had to choose where I would spend my time, and with whom.

I had to start noticing where I felt drained—and what was causing it.

This became my signal: the *empathic energy exchange.*

When energy is flowing both ways—mutual, reciprocal —the relationship feels balanced. Nourishing. Whole.

But when the energy is one-sided, it becomes a leak.

And in those moments, I learned:

- *I can still love you.*

- *I can still hold empathy.*
- *But I don't have to entangle myself in your experience to prove it.*

Empathy doesn't require entanglement.

It requires presence, awareness and discernment.

Returning to Wholeness – Healing the Shadow of Empathy

The shadow of empathy is not something to be ashamed of; it's something to bring into the light.

Whether it shows up as over-absorbing, over-fixing, or emotional numbness, these patterns are simply signs: your system needs *support, boundaries, and rest.*

My own journey showed me this truth—and maybe yours is showing you, too.

The work of reclaiming empathy is not to stop feeling, but to learn how to feel *with Grace - Gentleness, Reverence, Acceptance, Compassion, and Empathy.*

You can still be deeply empathetic and say no.

You can still care and walk away.

You can still feel with others without disappearing inside their pain.

This is what it means to be an empowered empath:

- Rooted. Sovereign. Awake.
- Present with others *and* present with yourself.

The Circle of Sovereignty

This is a grounding practice for empaths and highly sensitive people to reclaim their energy, reestablish emotional boundaries, and reconnect with their center—without shutting down their sensitivity.

You can do this ritual daily, after emotionally intense conversations, or anytime you feel drained or energetically "off."

Begin

Find a quiet space. Light a candle or sit by a window if possible. Close your eyes. Breathe slowly and deeply into your body. Let yourself arrive fully.

Say aloud or silently:

"I honor my ability to feel deeply. I release what is not mine. I return to myself."

Step 1: Call Your Energy Home

Visualize your energy as golden threads stretched out in different directions—threads that connect you to people, conversations, places, thoughts, and emotional interactions. You don't need to judge them—just notice.

Now gently call those threads back.

"Wherever I have left myself, I now return."

Picture the energy being drawn back into your heart space.

With each inhale, you gather yourself in.

With each exhale, you release what is not yours.

Step 2: Create Your Circle

Now imagine a glowing circle of light forming around you; an energetic boundary. This is your **Circle of Sovereignty.** It is permeable to love and truth, but it filters out projection, guilt, and energetic clutter.

Feel it forming at the edge of your aura, around your body.

Say:

"This is my sacred space. What is mine, stays. What is not mine, dissolves."

You may even anoint your heart, third eye, or the soles of your feet with essential oil or simply touch them as a blessing.

Step 3: Ground & Clear

Place your hands over your heart and ask:

"Whose energy is this?"

If it's yours; breathe, journal, and tend to it with kindness.

If it's not; visualize it draining down your legs, through your feet, and into the earth, where it can be transmuted into light.

Repeat until you feel clear and grounded.

Affirmations for Integration:

Speak aloud or write these in your journal:

- *I can feel deeply without losing myself.*
- *I am responsible for my energy; not everyone else's emotions.*
- *I am sovereign, sensitive, and safe.*
- *Empathy is my gift, and I use it with grace.*

Reflection – Nourishing Empathy Without Losing Yourself

- Where in my life does empathy feel nourishing and energizing?
- Where do I feel drained and what boundary is asking to be honored there?
- When have I confused empathy with over-responsibility?
- What part of me most needs empathy right now, and how can I offer it?

Closing Blessing: For the Sensitive Soul

May you feel deeply without drowning.

May you care without carrying.

May your empathy lead you to connection, not depletion.

May your nervous system feel safe to soften.

May your sensitivity become your strength.

And may you always remember:

Empathy is not weakness; it is Grace, embodied.

Where the Journey Deepens

Empathy asks us to feel deeply. To stay soft in a world that often demands we harden. And now, as we close this final chapter on the heart of Grace, I want to honor you for your willingness to explore such depth within yourself.

You've journeyed through Gentleness, Reverence, Acceptance, Compassion, and now, Empathy.

Each one of these elements holds a key.

Each one invites you home.

However, this is not the end.

What you've just completed is not a final destination—it is a sacred turning point. A threshold. The edge of something new.

What lies ahead is not a return to who you were before you began, but the unfolding of who you truly are.

Let us now step across this threshold together.

Living the Heart of Grace

Dear Traveler,

Congratulations. You are crossing the finish line of this book, but it's not the end of your journey.

If anything, this moment marks a sacred beginning.

You've walked through shadow and light. You've met hidden parts of yourself—some wounded, some waiting, all worthy. You've gathered tools, sat in reflection, and opened your heart to something ancient yet tenderly new: *Grace.*

And now, Grace walks with you.

It lives within your voice, your choices, your relationships, and your becoming.

This wasn't just a journey to understand Grace—it was a return to your deepest Self.

It was a reclamation of your worth, with Grace as your compass and companion.

Take a breath and honor this becoming.

You made it.

You're here.

You're ready.

Grace and Grace alone will set you free

At the very beginning of this journey, I offered five reflections about Grace. Four were explored. But one remained... quiet. Waiting.

"Grace, and Grace alone, will set us free."

I didn't explain it then because I hadn't fully lived it yet.

But now I have.

And now, I can tell you this:

Grace has, indeed, set me free.

Not all at once.

But gently.

Steadily.

Through every moment I stayed instead of running.

Through every breath that softened shame.

Through every truth I spoke aloud.

Through every tear I refused to silence.

Grace unhooked me from the lie that I had to earn love.

It returned me to belonging; not in someone else's eyes, but in my own.

That is freedom.

For me, Grace created freedom in:

- How I speak to myself in silence
- How I hold space for my pain without turning away
- How I receive love—guilt free, wide open
- How I trust my inner voice as sacred, not suspicious
- How I honor the wholeness of my being

May Grace do the same for you.

This stamp marks your sacred arrival. You've walked
the inner terrain with courage and care. May Grace
forever guide your way.

A Final Word from My Heart to Yours

Dear One,

Thank you for walking this path with me.

Not just reading; but *feeling*, remembering, releasing, reclaiming.

As I wrote these pages, I wasn't just offering you teachings; I was healing, too.

Grace didn't simply flow through my pen; it moved through my bones. It touched the places I thought were too far gone.

And maybe, just maybe, it touched something in you, too.

This book is not just a message from my guides. It is a love letter from one soul to another.

From one woman who needed Grace…

to another who's discovering it within herself.

Please remember this:

You are a treasure.

You are not too much or not enough—you are *exactly right*.

You are worthy of tenderness, of joy, of space to unfold.

The elements of Grace—Gentleness, Reverence, Acceptance, Compassion, and Empathy already live inside you.

When the world forgets who you are, when *you* forget who you are—reach inward.

You'll find them there.

You'll find *you* there.

You are more than enough.

You are a miracle, still unfolding.

With so much love,

Shelly

Your Next Steps: Walking Deeper with Grace

If this journey has stirred something within you, an awakening, a remembering, and you're feeling called to go deeper, I invite you to continue this sacred path with me.

I've created a soul-nurturing group experience called *The Passport to Grace*—a nurturing container where we deepen the embodiment of self-love using the five elements of the heart of Grace. Through weekly soul practices, guided meditations, intuitive journaling, and creative expression, you'll be supported in anchoring these teachings into your daily life. In our first session we will start with the **Soul Star Activation**—a powerful energetic initiation designed to awaken and align the inner light of each Grace element already within you. This sacred circle is a space where your heart will be held, your voice honored, and your growth celebrated.

If you're not quite ready to step into the full group experience but still feel called to begin, the **Soul Star Activation** is also available as a self-guided digital journey or as a private one-on-one virtual experience with me. This guided energetic practice will gently awaken and align you with the five elements of Grace—offering a beautiful entry point into your own sacred unfolding.

Scan the QR code below to learn more and sign up:

https://www.journeytotheheartofgrace.com/

I'd Love to Hear from You

Whether you're still walking with these teachings or letting them settle in your soul, your voice matters.

If you feel inspired to share how this journey impacted you, I welcome your words—whether it's a personal message, a testimonial, or a review. Your reflection might help someone else find the courage to begin their own path toward self-love through Grace.

Your voice is sacred here.

I'm honored to have been a part of your journey.

Link: https://form.jotform.com/251537833515863

ABOUT THE AUTHOR

Shelly Van Goeye is a Soul Rejuvenation Coach, artist, and international bestselling author who guides others on sacred inner journeys of self-love, healing, and transformation. With a unique blend of shadow work, spiritual insight, and creative expression, she helps people release what weighs them down and reconnect with their true worth through grace-filled practices and soulful embodiment.

Her debut book, *Journey to the Heart of Grace: A Self-Love Survival Guide*, is a reflection of her own path of unlearning self-abandonment, healing from betrayal, and returning to wholeness. Rooted in her lived experience and professional expertise, Shelly's work invites readers into a gentle yet radical reframe: that grace, when turned inward, becomes self-love—and self-love changes everything.

Her signature framework—*the five elements to the heart of Grace*: Gentleness, Reverence, Acceptance, Compassion, and Empathy—offers a powerful pathway back to self, serving as both compass and companion for the soul-weary seeking home within themselves. Through her writing, coaching, and art, Shelly creates spaces of transformation and truth, where healing becomes possible and creativity becomes a form of communion.

When not writing, coaching, or painting in her studio, Shelly finds inspiration hiking with her dogs, soaking in nature, and sharing meaningful conversations with those she loves. She lives in Holland, Michigan, and continues to find beauty in color, connection, and quiet moments of grace.

Learn more about Shelly and her work at:

www.shellyvangoeye.com.

www.ingramcontent.com/pod-product-compliance
Lightning Source LLC
Chambersburg PA
CBHW071442090426
42737CB00011B/1754